Finish Line for ELLs

English Proficiency Practice

Continental Press

Credits

Illustrations by Carolyn Williams and Laurie Conley

Photos: Cover and title page: *boy on scooter and tug of war,* Radius/Punchstock; *girl on rope swing and patty cake,* Corbis/Punchstock

Continental Press, Inc. and the *Finish Line for ELLs* materials are neither affiliated with nor endorsed by any collaborative state organization.

ISBN 978-0-8454-5834-1

Table of Contents

About *Finish Line for ELLs: English Proficiency Practice*

The *Finish Line for ELLs: English Proficiency Practice* workbook was developed to help teachers prepare English language learners in grade 1 for similar items found on English language proficiency assessments, such as ACCESS for ELLs® test developed by the WIDA® Consortium, ELDA, NYSESLAT, and individual state tests based on the TESOL standards. By using this workbook, students will become familiar with the types of questions they will face on testing day: multiple choice, written response, and oral response. The book is divided into four units, each one addressing a language domain: speaking, listening, reading, and writing. The content in the listening, reading, and writing units is written for students with developing proficiency levels, overlapping the intermediate, intermediate high, and advanced levels. The lessons in the speaking unit use adaptive questioning to move through five proficiency levels: beginner, intermediate, intermediate high, advanced, and advanced high.

Each unit begins with a model problem to work through with the students. The lessons in each unit are organized by theme folder, each one addressing a specific context for language acquisition: conversational language, academic language arts, academic mathematics, academic science, and academic social studies.

Unit	Basic Format	Question Type	Scoring
Listening	Students listen to information read by the teacher or on an audio CD and then answer questions.	Multiple choice	• Fill in responses in book or use answer sheets
Reading	Students read sentences or passages and respond to questions.	Multiple choice	• Fill in responses in book or use answer sheets
Writing	Students read text and use graphics to formulate ideas in order to write answers to constructed response questions.	Written response	• Write answers to questions in book • Rubrics provided in back of teacher's edition
Speaking	Students use graphic clues to help them speak in response to questions asked by the teacher.	Oral response	• Scored by teacher during administration • Rubrics provided in back of teacher's edition

An accompanying annotated teacher's edition provides answer keys, directions for administering each lesson, and comprehensive skill activities to provide even more practice. Additional teacher support materials in the Appendix include: parent letters in multiple languages, answer sheets with rubrics, and a chart that connects the skills addressed in each unit to workbooks developed by Continental Press that may be used to extend practice to promote English language proficiency.

WIDA and ACCESS for ELLs are registered trademarks of the Board of Regents of the University of Wisconsin System.

Each lesson in this unit focuses on a specific content topic:

1. Conversational language
2. The language of Academic Language Arts
3. The language of Academic Mathematics
4. The language of Academic Science
5. The language of Academic Social Studies

In this unit, you will:

- read and listen to a short story about a picture told in familiar language
- listen to a question
- make out key words in the question
- keep the question in your mind
- listen to and read answer choices
- use picture clues to answer a question
- mark the correct answer

Listen carefully and try to do the best you can!

Model Lesson

At the Pet Store

1.

2. (A) A kitten

   (B) A rabbit

   (C) A puppy

   (D) A bird

Crossing the Street Safely

Safety Rules

1.

Ⓐ　　　　　Ⓑ　　　　　Ⓒ

2.

Ⓐ　　　　　Ⓑ　　　　　Ⓒ

3.

(A)

(B)

(C)

4.

(A)

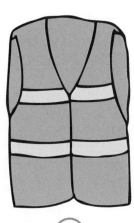

(B)

(C)

Gifts for Grandma

1.

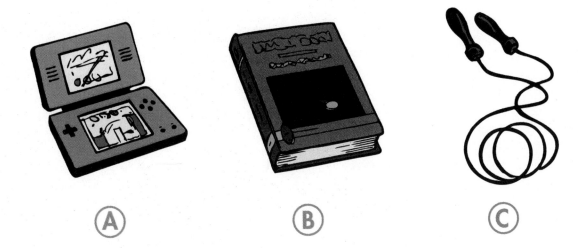

Ⓐ   Ⓑ   Ⓒ

2.

 Ⓐ   Ⓑ   Ⓒ

3.

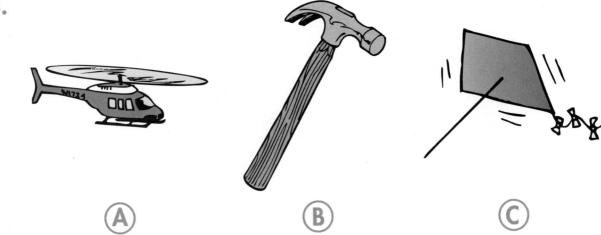

Ⓐ   Ⓑ   Ⓒ

4.

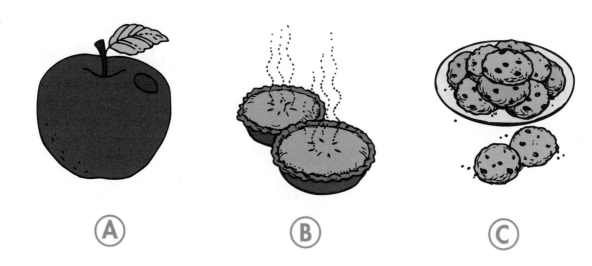

How Many Animals?

NATURE MUSEUM

Quantity

1.

(A)

(B)

(C)

2.

Ⓐ

Ⓑ

Ⓒ

Quantity

3.

FOLDER C

Quantity

4.

(A)

(B)

(C)

Meet Johnny Appleseed

1.

Ⓐ   Ⓑ   Ⓒ

2.

(A)

(B)

(C)

Historical Figures

3.

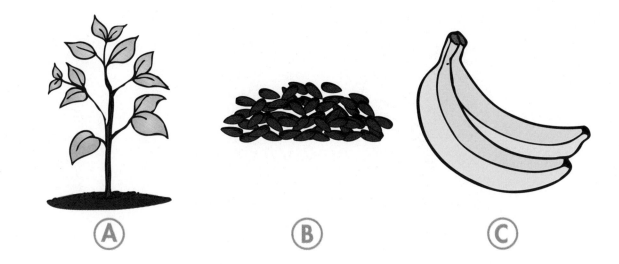

Ⓐ   Ⓑ   Ⓒ

4.

Ⓐ

Ⓑ

Ⓒ

Living and Nonliving Things

Living and Nonliving Things

1.

Ⓐ   Ⓑ   Ⓒ

FOLDER
E

Living and Nonliving Things

2.

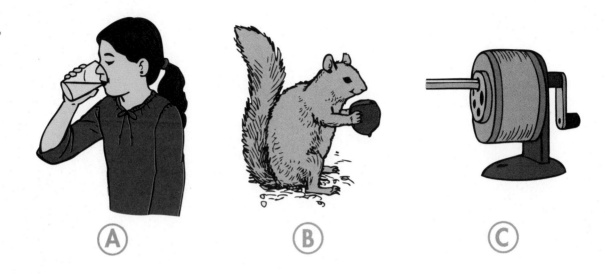

Ⓐ　　　　Ⓑ　　　　Ⓒ

Living and Nonliving Things

3. (A) A 🧑 can grow.

(B) A 📱 can grow.

(C) A 🌹 can grow.

4.

Ⓐ It can see.

Ⓑ It is big.

Ⓒ It likes the water.

Ⓓ It can move by itself.

Playground Fun

Leisure Activities

1.

 Ⓐ

 Ⓑ

 Ⓒ

2.

 Ⓐ

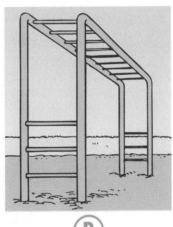 Ⓑ

 Ⓒ

3.

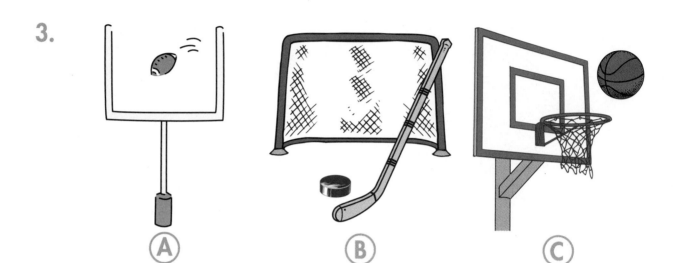

Ⓐ   Ⓑ   Ⓒ

4.

Ⓐ   Ⓑ   Ⓒ

Mother Goose Rhymes

1.

Ⓐ

Ⓑ

Ⓒ

2.

3. (A) After

   (B) Jack

   (C) Water

   (D) Hill

4. (A) One, shoe

   (B) Four, door

   (C) Five, pick

   (D) Ten, big

What's My Size?

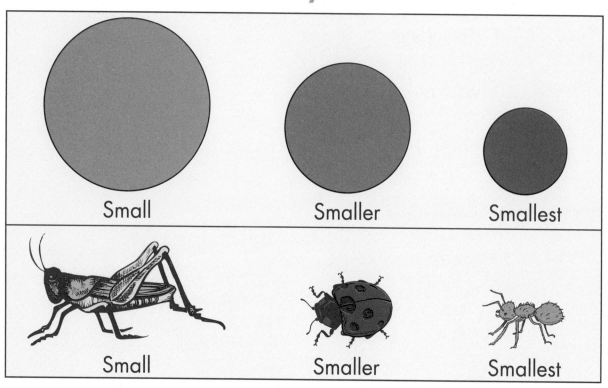

Small   Smaller   Smallest

Small   Smaller   Smallest

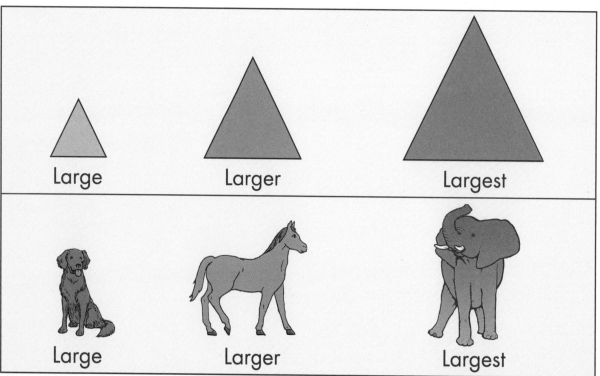

Large   Larger   Largest

Large   Larger   Largest

Size

1.

Ⓐ

Ⓑ

Ⓒ

2.

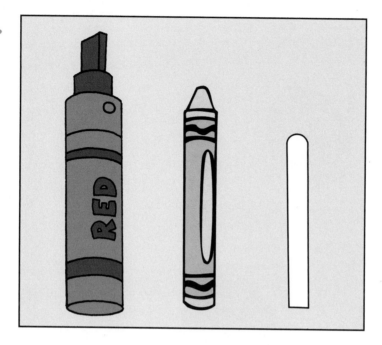

(A)

(B)

(C)

FOLDER C — Size

3.

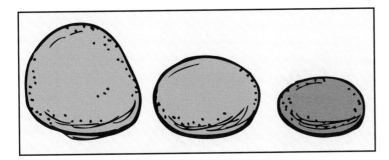

 A

B

C

4.

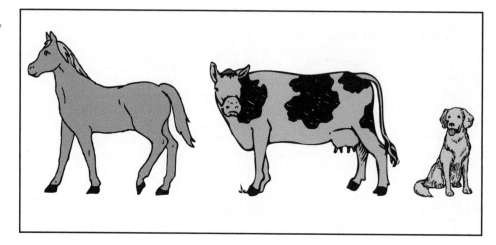

(A) A 🐕 is larger than a 🐴 .

(B) A 🐕 is larger than a 🐄 .

(C) A 🐄 is larger than a 🐴 .

(D) A 🐴 is larger than a 🐕 .

FOLDER D

Neighborhoods and Communities

A Neighborhood Map

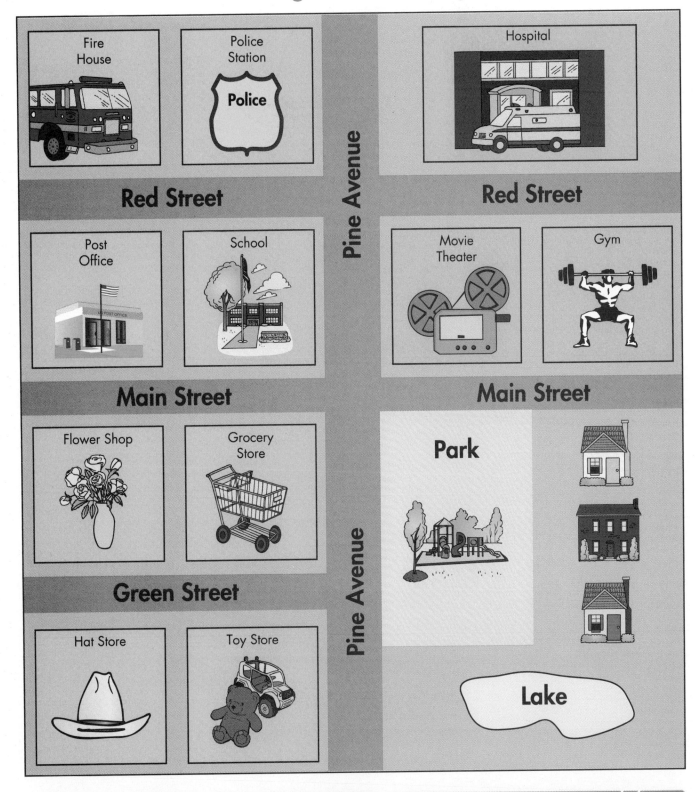

Neighborhoods and Communities

1.

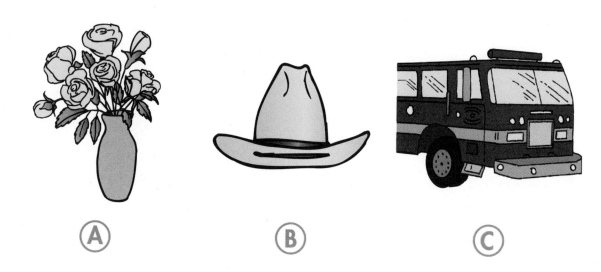

Ⓐ   Ⓑ   Ⓒ

Neighborhoods and Communities

2. Ⓐ The police station

   Ⓑ The grocery store

   Ⓒ The gym

   Ⓓ The hospital

3. Ⓐ "It is across the street from the school."

   Ⓑ "It is next to the hospital."

   Ⓒ "It is to the left of the gym."

   Ⓓ "It is at Green Street and Pine Avenue."

4. (A) "The school is near the toy store."

(B) "The flower store is across the street from the police station."

(C) "The post office is next to the hat store."

(D) "The park is next to the lake."

The Weather

| Cloudy | Rainy | Sunny | Windy | Snowy |

1.

(A)

(B)

(C)

(D)

2.

(A) Cool

(B) Hot

(C) Cold

(D) Warm

FOLDER
E

Weather

3.

(A) It is a cloudy day.

(B) It is a windy day.

(C) It is a sunny day.

(D) It is a rainy day.

4.

(A) It is cool and cloudy.

(B) It is cold and snowy.

(C) It is warm and rainy.

(D) It is hot and sunny.

Each lesson in this unit focuses on a specific content topic:

1. Conversational language
2. The language of Academic Language Arts
3. The language of Academic Mathematics
4. The language of Academic Science
5. The language of Academic Social Studies

In this unit, you will:

- read a chart or short story with several paragraphs
- understand questions about the text
- use picture clues and key words to answer questions about
  - reading graphic organizers
  - identifying whole numbers
  - comparing and contrasting
  - understanding sequence
  - finding main idea and details
  - making predictions
  - understanding vocabulary
- mark the correct answer

Read carefully and try to do the best you can!

Caring for Pets

What We Will Do	Kind of Pet	Times
Play with String	Kittens	11:00 A.M.–11:30 A.M.
Feed the Animals	Rabbits	12:00 noon–12:30 P.M.
Play with a Ball	Puppies	1:00 P.M.–1:30 P.M.
Give a Bath	Puppies	1:00 P.M.–1:30 P.M.

1. Melissa wants to help feed the rabbits. Look at the chart. What time will she need to be at the store for that event?

   (A) 11:00 A.M.

   (B) 12 noon

   (C) 1:30 P.M.

2. Look at the schedule of events at the pet store. What sentence tells something true about the show schedule?

(A) All of the events happen at the same time.

(B) Only the puppies have play time.

(C) The puppies play and get baths during the same time.

(D) There are no events at the store after 12 noon.

Let's Read!

Anna asks Mike, "Where do you want to sit?"

Mike answers, "I want to sit on the sofa."

Anna and Mike sit on the sofa.

Anna has a book of stories. She asks Mike, "What do you want to read about?"

Mike says, "I want to read about an animal!"

Anna reads a story about an animal.

Mike claps his hands. Mike smiles at Anna.

Likes and Dislikes

1. Where do Anna and Mike sit?

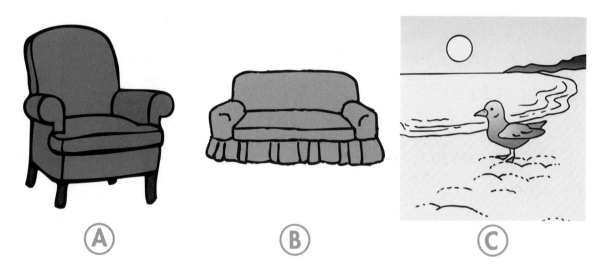

Ⓐ　　　　　　　　Ⓑ　　　　　　　　Ⓒ

2. What does Mike want to read about?

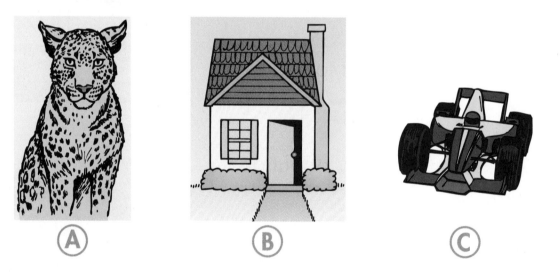

Ⓐ　　　　　　　　Ⓑ　　　　　　　　Ⓒ

3. How does Mike feel?

    (A) Mike feels mad.

    (B) Mike feels sad.

    (C) Mike feels happy.

Money

Coins, Coins, Coins

A penny is one cent.

A nickel is five cents. Five pennies equal one nickel.

A dime is ten cents. Ten pennies equal one dime.

A quarter is twenty-five cents. Twenty-five pennies equal one quarter.

A half-dollar is fifty cents. Fifty pennies equal one half-dollar.

A dollar is one hundred cents. One hundred pennies equal one dollar.

Penny One cent 1¢

Nickel Five cents 5¢

Dime Ten cents 10¢

Quarter Twenty-five cents 25¢

Half-dollar Fifty cents 50¢

Dollar One hundred cents 100¢

FOLDER B

Money

1. Look at the pictures of the coins. Which coin is a dime?

Ⓐ   Ⓑ   Ⓒ

2. Look at the pictures of the coins. Which coin is a quarter?

Ⓐ   Ⓑ   Ⓒ

3. Read the passage on page 64 again. Which coin is the same as 50 pennies?

Ⓐ   Ⓑ   Ⓒ

Money

4. Read the passage on page 64 again. Which coins equal the same amount of money?

FOLDER C

Organisms and Environment

A Walk in the Forest

Meg looks up. "Look at the tall trees! The leaves have many colors. Some are red. Some are orange. Some are yellow. Some are green."

Mom says, "Leaves change over the year. In the winter, there are no leaves on most of the trees. In the spring, new leaves grow. In the summer, the leaves get bigger. In the fall, some leaves turn colors and fall off. Some trees have green leaves all year."

Mom says, "The ground is called the forest floor."

Meg asks, "What is this plant?"

Mom says, "This is a fern. Ferns look like green feathers. They grow under trees."

Meg asks, "What is this? It is a rug on the forest floor!"

Mom says, "That is moss. Moss is soft, thick green plants."

Meg looks up and down. She says, "I see squirrels looking for nuts. I see birds in the trees. I see bugs crawling on the ground."

Meg says, "I like to walk in the forest. There is a lot to see."

FOLDER
C

Organisms and Environment

1. Which picture shows a tree in the fall?

Ⓐ   Ⓑ   Ⓒ   Ⓓ

2. Which picture shows a forest plant?

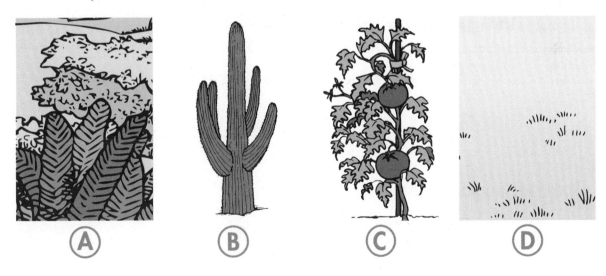

Ⓐ   Ⓑ   Ⓒ   Ⓓ

Organisms and Environment

3. Read this sentence.

    Brown leaves are on the ground in the forest.

    What word means "the ground in the forest"?

    (A) Fire

    (B) Floor

    (C) Flower

    (D) Flat

4. What does moss look like?

    (A) It looks like brown leaves.

    (B) It looks like a feather.

    (C) It looks like a tree.

    (D) It looks like a green rug.

Sequence

Time Order Words

Play Ball!

First, Miguel pats Red on the head. Next, Miguel throws the ball. Last, Red brings the ball to Miguel.

First

Next

Last

Kitty and the Fish

First, Kitty looks at the fish. Next, Kitty tries to get the fish. Last, Tom tells Kitty to go away.

First

Next

Last

The New Kite

First, Ming and Lee make a kite. Next, they fly the kite. Last, the kite gets stuck in the tree.

First

Next

Last

Sequence

1. Read "Play Ball!" on page 71 again.
    What happens <u>last</u>?

Ⓐ   Ⓑ   Ⓒ

2. Read "Kitty and the Fish" on page 71 again.
    What happens <u>first</u>?

Ⓐ   Ⓑ   Ⓒ

3. Which is the correct time order for the words below?

　　(A) Next, Last, First

　　(B) First, Next, Last

　　(C) Last, First, Next

4. Read the sentences below.

　　First, Ming and Lee make a kite.

　　_____, they fly the kite.

　　Last, the kite gets stuck in the tree.

Which word goes in the sentence?

　　(A) Finally

　　(B) Third

　　(C) When

　　(D) Next

U.S. Symbols

The flag of the United States has seven red stripes. Red means brave. The flag has six white stripes. White means good. Part of the flag is blue. Blue means fair. The flag has 50 stars, too. There is one star for each state. You see the flag at schools. You see it flying in front of buildings. You can see it in many places.

The bald eagle is the U.S. bird. The eagle is a big, strong bird. It has strong wings. The eagle flies high in the sky. It looks so free!

Uncle Sam stands for the U.S. Uncle Sam wears red and white striped pants. His coat is blue. His tall hat has stars on it. There are pictures of Uncle Sam. You can see people dressed as Uncle Sam in a parade.

FOLDER
E

Cultural Heritage

1. Which flag is the U.S. flag?

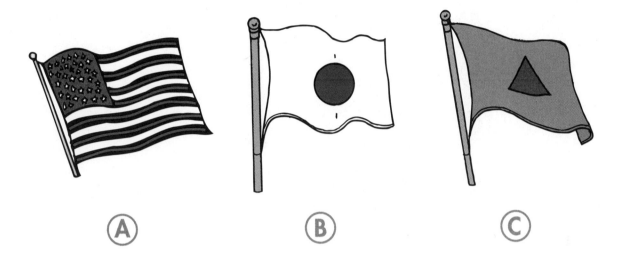

Ⓐ   Ⓑ   Ⓒ

2. What do Uncle Sam's clothes look like?

    Ⓐ They look like a sheet.

    Ⓑ They look like a bird.

    Ⓒ They look like the U.S. flag.

    Ⓓ They look like a red bag.

3. Why is the eagle the U.S. bird?

    (A) It is little.

    (B) It is strong.

    (C) It is funny.

    (D) It is happy.

Rosa Helps

Dad says, "Rosa, please read a story to your little brother."

Rosa says, "Yes, Dad. I will read to Juan. It's fun to help you."

Rosa reads a story to Juan. Juan looks at the pictures.

Dad smiles at the children.

Mom says, "It's time for lunch. Rosa, please put the plates on the table."

Rosa says, "Yes, Mom. I like to help you."

Mom says, "Thank you, Rosa. I am glad you help me."

After lunch, Juan says, "Rosa, please push me on the swing."

Rosa says, "Sure, Juan. I will push you very high. You will have a good time."

Mom and Dad say, "Thank you, Rosa. You are a good helper."

Sharing and Cooperation

1. Read the story on page 77 again. Which picture shows Rosa helping her family?

Ⓐ   Ⓑ   Ⓒ

2. Read the story on page 77 again. Which sentence says that Rosa helps her family?

Ⓐ Rosa reads a story to Juan.

Ⓑ Juan likes the pictures.

Ⓒ Dad smiles.

Ⓓ It's time for lunch.

3. Read the story on page 77 again. Mom says, "Rosa, please put away the food." Rosa wants to help. What does she say?

(A) "No. I don't want to do that."

(B) "May I go out to play?"

(C) "Okay. I will help you now."

(D) "Maybe after I take a nap."

Bead Patterns

A pattern is something that goes over and over again. Look at the shapes below. Do you see the pattern? The pattern is one round bead, one square bead, one long bead. Then the pattern starts again.

A pattern can have different numbers of things. Look at the shapes below. Do you see the pattern? The pattern is one round bead, two square beads, two long beads. Then the pattern starts again.

You can tell what comes next in a pattern. Name each shape. Count how many beads of each shape you see. What is the pattern?

The pattern is one long bead, two square beads, three round beads. Your pattern looks like this:

FOLDER B Patterns

1. Which drawing shows a pattern?

   Ⓐ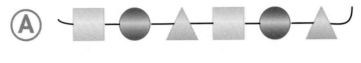

   Ⓑ

   Ⓒ

2. Read the story on page 80 again. A *pattern* is something that

   Ⓐ Is always the same

   Ⓑ Happens over and over

   Ⓒ Is different every time

   Ⓓ Is funny

3. Look at the pattern below. What comes next?

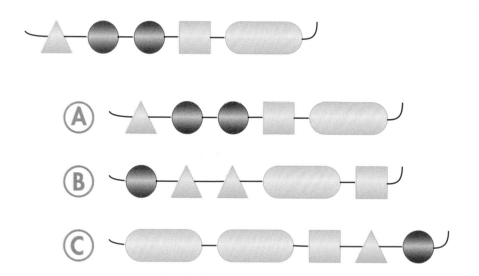

4. Look at the pattern below. What comes next?

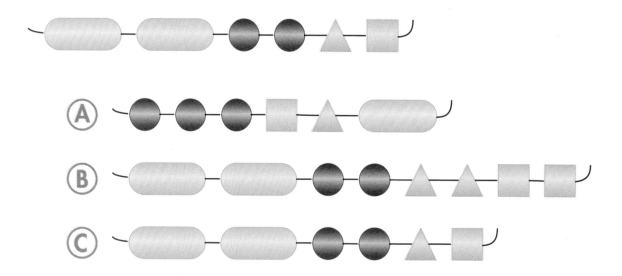

Birds

A bird is an animal. A bird has wings and a tail. A bird has two eyes and two ears. A bird's mouth is called a bill or beak. It uses the beak to catch food.

Some birds eat bugs. Their beaks are thin. Their beaks have points. They can poke their beaks into little holes where bugs live. Some birds eat seeds. Their beaks are short. They can crack the seeds.

Ducks live near the water. They get food in the water. Some ducks eat plants. They have wide bills. Wide bills help the ducks pull plants from the water. Other ducks have long, thin bills. These ducks eat fish. Long, narrow bills help them catch fish.

Owls hear and see very well. They hunt at night. Owls eat mice and other small animals. An owl has a sharp beak. The beak has hooks on it. An owl sees or hears a mouse. The owl flies down to the mouse. Sharp claws grab the mouse. The hooked beak grabs the mouse. The owl eats its food.

Animals

1. Which picture shows a bird?

Ⓐ

Ⓑ

Ⓒ

2. A bird's mouth is called a beak or a

Ⓐ Tail

Ⓑ Wing

Ⓒ Bill

Ⓓ Claw

3. Some ducks eat plants. What are their bills like?

   (A) They are thin.

   (B) They are short.

   (C) They are sharp.

   (D) They are wide.

4. An eagle has a beak. It looks like an owl's beak. What does an eagle eat?

   (A) An eagle eats meat.

   (B) An eagle eats grass.

   (C) An eagle eats flowers.

   (D) An eagle eats fruit.

Playtime

Patty and Mia went out to play.

It was a pretty, sunny day.

Patty threw the ball.

It did not fall.

Mia saw the cloud.

She said out loud,

"I see a drop.

We have to stop."

Into the house the two girls came.

They sat on the rug to play a game.

The friends were glad.

They were not sad.

1. The words *ball* and *fall* are in the same word family. Which picture stands for another word in the same word family?

Ⓐ   Ⓑ   Ⓒ

2. The words *play* and *day* are in the same word family. Which word is in the same word family?

    Ⓐ Please

    Ⓑ Stay

    Ⓒ Dog

    Ⓓ Wave

3. The words *drop* and *stop* are in the same word family. Which word is <u>not</u> in the same word family?

　　Ⓐ Top

　　Ⓑ Pop

　　Ⓒ Hop

　　Ⓓ Rope

4. The words *game* and *came* are in the same word family. Which word is <u>not</u> in the same word family?

　　Ⓐ Fame

　　Ⓑ Tame

　　Ⓒ Clam

　　Ⓓ Name

Where Do Animals Live?

Beavers build their homes in rivers or streams. The home is called a lodge. A lodge is made from sticks, leaves, and mud. Some of the lodge is under the water. Most of the lodge is above the water. The beavers swim under the water. They go into the lodge. They are safe there.

Some animals live in caves. A cave is a hole in the rocks. The hole can be big or little. A cave can keep animals safe. Bats live in dark caves. They hang by their feet. Bears sleep in caves. Caves keep bears warm and dry. Crabs live in caves. Those caves are under the water.

Some animals live in trees. Birds build nests in trees. Monkeys build nests in trees. They make nests from sticks and leaves. Squirrels live in trees. They store nuts and other food in trees. Owls live in holes in trees. Some snakes live in trees, too. Bees live in hives that hang in trees. Trees keep these animals safe.

Homes and Habitats

1. Which picture shows a beaver lodge?

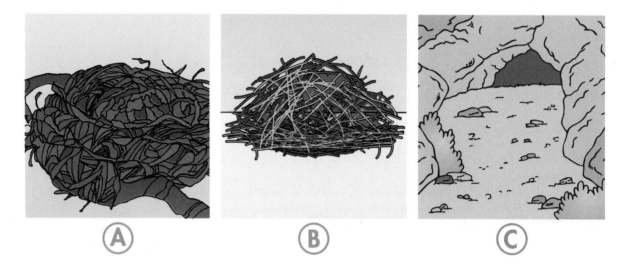

Ⓐ   Ⓑ   Ⓒ

Homes and Habitats

2. Where do bats, bears, and crabs live?

   (A) Trees

   (B) Nests

   (C) Caves

   (D) Hives

3. How is a lodge like a nest?

   (A) They are both up in trees.

   (B) They are both under the water.

   (C) They are both made with sticks.

   (D) They are both made with rocks.

4. Which sentence is <u>not</u> true?

    Ⓐ All animal homes are in trees.

    Ⓑ Homes keep animals safe.

    Ⓒ Animals store food in their homes.

    Ⓓ Homes keep animals warm and dry.

Each lesson in this unit focuses on a specific content topic or topics:

1. Conversational language
2. The language of Academic Language Arts
3. The language of Academic Mathematics
4. The language of Academic Science
5. The language of Academic Social Studies

In this unit, you will:

- read a chart or short story with pictures
- understand questions about the text
- use picture clues and key words to answer questions about the text
- use information in the stories, pictures, and questions to get ideas for writing about a topic
- write ideas as notes
- write about the topic in clear and complete sentences

Write neatly and try to do the best you can!

The Needs of Living Things

Animals are living things. Plants are living things. All living things have basic needs in order to survive. Animals need air, water, food, and shelter. Plants need air, water, nutrients, and light. When we take care of animals or plants, we must give them the things they need to help them survive.

Living Things—Animals

Living Things—Plants

Now it's time to write!

What do plants and animals need to survive? Write a paragraph about taking care of living things. If you have cared for an animal or plant, write about your experience. Tell what you need to do to help a pet or a plant survive.

_____

_____

_____

_____

_____

_____

_____

Check your writing. Ask yourself:

- ☐ Does my writing make sense?
- ☐ Did I write in complete sentences?
- ☐ Did I use correct punctuation and spelling?

Feelings and Emotions

Atiya flies her kite.

Atiya feels happy.

Feelings and Emotions

Now it's time to write!

Write about 3 things you do. Tell how they make you feel.

1. I _____.

   I feel _____.

2. _____.

   _____.

3. _____.

   _____.

Check your writing. Ask yourself:

☐ Does my writing make sense?

☐ Did I write in complete sentences?

☐ Did I use correct punctuation and spelling?

Favorite Fruits

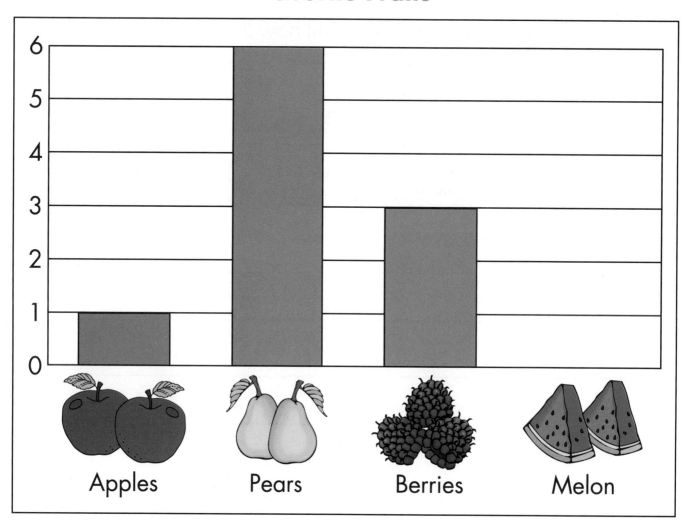

Luis wrote what he learned from his graph.

One friend likes apples.

Three friends like berries.

No one likes melon.

Pears are the favorite fruit.

I will take pears to our picnic.

FOLDER B

Interpreting Data

Now it's time to write!

Jill is having a party. She asks her friends which ice cream flavors they like. She makes a graph. Write 3 sentences to tell what the graph shows.

Use the graph below and the model on page 98 to help you. Write your answer on the next page.

Ice Cream Favorites

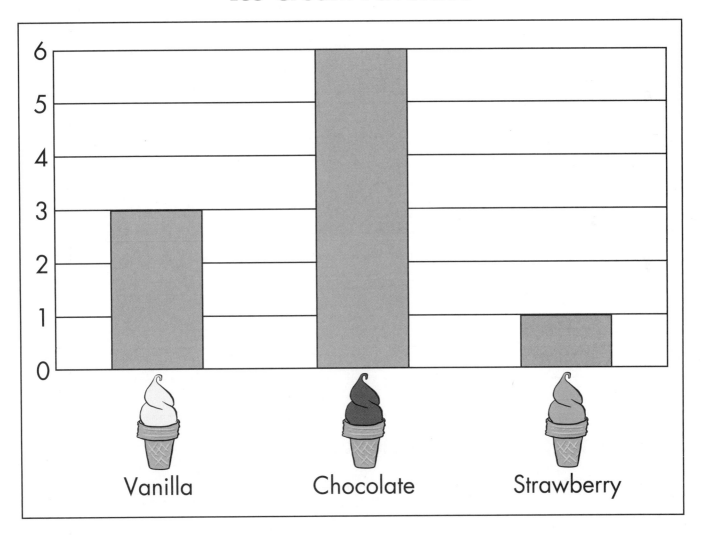

Interpreting Data

_____

_____

_____

_____

_____

_____

_____

_____

_____

_____

_____

_____

Check your writing. Ask yourself:

☐ Does my writing make sense?

☐ Did I write in complete sentences?

☐ Did I use correct punctuation and spelling?

Animals

Marco writes about penguins.
First, he draws a penguin.
He writes the words for the body parts.
Then he writes what he learned.

Penguin

Bill

Eye

Neck

Flipper-like wing

Belly

Back

Webbed feet

Wedge-shaped tail

Claws

A penguin has two eyes.

A penguin has a bill.

A penguin has two webbed feet.

Animals

Now it's time to write!

Look at this picture of a dog. Label some of the dog's body parts. Then write 3 sentences about the dog's body parts.

_____

_____

_____

_____

_____

Check your writing. Ask yourself:

☐ Does my writing make sense?

☐ Did I write in complete sentences?

☐ Did I use correct punctuation and spelling?

Emma wants to write a book about seasons.
She wants to tell facts about seasons.
She wants to make the book fun to read.
She wants to write a pattern book.

I am a warm, rainy season.
I make flowers grow.
People like to have picnics in my season.
What season am I?

I am a hot season.
I make vegetables grow.
People like to swim in my season.
What season am I?

Now it's time to write!

Continue the pattern book that Emma started. Write about one of the other two seasons. Use the same pattern Emma used.

1   Get Ready to Write

Use these questions to get ideas.

What is another season?

What is the weather like?

What is special about this season?

What do people do in this season?

Turn to the next page to make a plan for writing.

2 Plan Your Writing

Look at the pictures. Draw a circle around the season you will write about. On the lines below, describe the season you will write about.

windy

3 Write Your Pattern Book

Write your pattern book on the next page. Use your answers to the questions on page 104 and the ideas you wrote on page 105 to help you.

When you are finished, remember to review the checklist on page 107. The questions are important. They will help you to do your best work.

I am a _____ season.

I make _____

_____.

People like _____

_____.

_____

_____?

Check your writing. Ask yourself:

☐ Did I tell about a season?

☐ Did I follow the pattern?

☐ Did I write in complete sentences?

☐ Did I use correct punctuation and spelling?

Personal Correspondence

Eva wrote an e-mail to her friend.

She wrote about what happened.

From: Eva
To: Lupe
Subject: My fun day

New   Send   Reply   Attach

Lupe,

    We played ball.
    It started to rain.
    We went inside.
    We played a game.

                    Eva

Personal Correspondence

Now it's time to write!

Look at the pictures of Nina. Help her write an e-mail to Bob to tell what happened.

Bob,

I saw _____

_____

_____

_____

Your friend,
Nina

Check your writing. Ask yourself:

☐ Does my writing make sense?

☐ Did I write in complete sentences?

☐ Did I use correct punctuation and spelling?

The Big Car Race!

Four cars had a race.

The car called Dash was second.

Jazz was third...

FOLDER B — Number Sense

Now it's time to write!

Look at the picture. Four children are standing in line. Write sentences to tell who is first, second, third, and last.

Use the picture below and the model on page 110 to help you. Write your answer on the next page.

_____

_____

_____

_____

_____

_____

_____

_____

_____

_____

_____

_____

Check your writing. Ask yourself:

☐ Does my writing make sense?

☐ Did I write in complete sentences?

☐ Did I use correct punctuation and spelling?

Stages of Growing

How a Frog Grows

Scientists watch animals grow. They use pictures and words to describe how animals grow.

Stages of a Frog

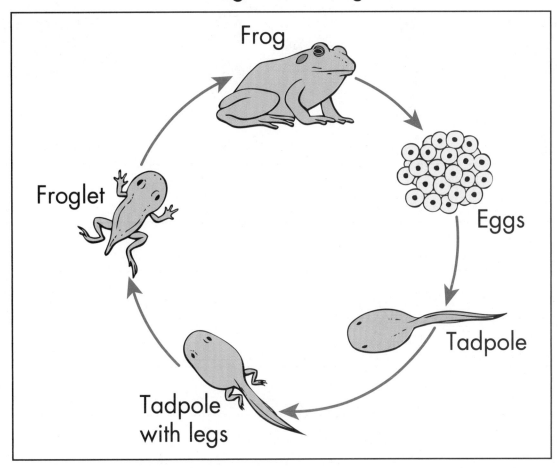

A scientist could use this chart to tell how a frog grows. Here is how a scientist might start.

A frog begins as a tiny, round egg. The egg turns into a tadpole.

A tadpole is long. It has a pointed tail. It has no legs. Then the

tadpole....

Stages of Growing

Now it's time to write!

Write at least 4 sentences about how a butterfly grows and changes. Tell how the butterfly looks at each stage.

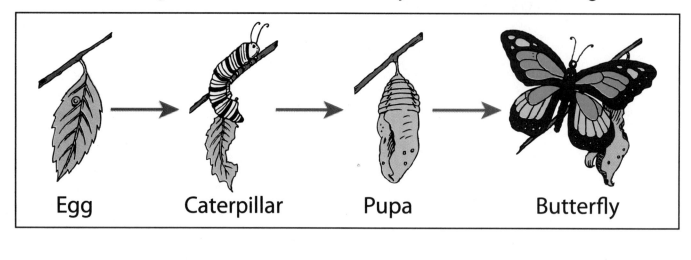

Egg   Caterpillar   Pupa   Butterfly

_____

_____

_____

_____

_____

_____

Check your writing. Ask yourself:

☐ Does my writing make sense?

☐ Did I write in complete sentences?

☐ Did I use correct punctuation and spelling?

The Race

Deer loved to brag. He told everyone how fast he could run. The animals got tired of listening to him. One day Snail said, "Do you want to race with me?"

Deer said, "Yes, I will race you! I will win, too! I am the fastest animal in the forest!"

1. Follow the main road out of town.
2. Turn right at the big, gray rock.
3. Turn left at the tree.
4. Cross the finish line.

All the animals came to watch the race. Owl read the directions to Deer and Snail.

Deer began to run. He ran so fast, he didn't see anything. He ran faster and faster. He didn't see the big rock. He didn't see the tree.

Snail walked slowly. He looked at everything carefully. He saw the rock. He turned right. He saw the tree. He turned left.

Snail crossed the finish line. All the animals cheered. Deer could not hear the cheers. He was lost in the woods.

LESSON: Winners follow directions.

Now it's time to write!

Think about the order that events happened in the story. Write a sequence chain to tell what happened to Deer and Snail.

1 Prepare Your Ideas

Use these questions to help you gather ideas for your writing.

What happens in the beginning?

What happens in the middle?

What happens in the end?

What did you learn from the story?

Turn to the next page to make a plan for writing.

2 Plan Your Writing

Put numbers by the events to tell what happened first, second, and third.

_____

_____

_____

3 Write Your Sequence Chain

Write a sequence chain about Deer and Snail on pages 119 and 120. Put one thing that happened in the story in each box. Then tell what you learned from the story. Use your own words. Use your answers to the questions on page 116 and the pictures on page 117 to help you.

When you are finished, remember to review the checklist on page 120. The questions are important. They will help you to do your best work.

First, _____

_____

_____

_____

↓

Then _____

_____

_____

_____

In the end, _____

_____

_____

_____

The lesson I learned is _____

_____

_____

_____

Check your writing. Ask yourself:

- ☐ Did I tell what happened in "The Race"?
- ☐ Did I tell the events in order?
- ☐ Did I write in complete sentences?
- ☐ Did I use correct punctuation and spelling?

Each lesson in this unit focuses on a specific content topic or topics:

1. Conversational language
2. The language of Academic Language Arts
3. The language of Academic Mathematics
4. The language of Academic Science
5. The language of Academic Social Studies

In this unit, you will:

- look at a picture or pictures
- find information and vocabulary in the picture
- listen to and understand a question asked by your teacher
- answer a series of questions about the pictures
- use the picture clues to help answer the questions

Speak clearly and try to do the best you can!

Likes and Dislikes

Part 1

There are many kinds of foods. Some foods taste good to you. You like those foods. Some foods do not taste good to you. You dislike those foods.

Part 2

Lunch A   Lunch B

We pick a meal that has mostly foods we like.
Sometimes, a meal may have some foods that we do not
like on the tray.

Part 3

Breakfast Menu

Main Dishes

Fried eggs   Pancakes   Waffles   Cereal

Side Dishes

Melon   Bananas   Potatoes

Beverages

Milk   Orange juice   Smoothie

People in the United States eat many kinds of foods for breakfast. When you go to a restaurant, you can choose the foods you like from a menu.

Part 1

Everyone has neighbors. Sometimes, neighbors live close together. Sometimes, neighbors live far apart.

Neighbors work together to make their neighborhood a good place to live.

Part 2

Neighbors read the newspaper.

They need to know about their neighborhood.

Neighbors go to meetings.

They talk about how to keep people safe.

Neighbors vote for leaders.

They choose strong, smart people.

These are things that grown-ups do to be good neighbors.

Part 3

You can be a good neighbor, too.

You can follow the rules for keeping safe.

There are many ways to be safe.

You can swim in places that have a lifeguard.

You can ask a police officer for help if you get lost.

You can call 911 if you are hurt or in trouble.

Part 4

There are many other ways that you can be a good neighbor.

You can throw garbage in a trash can, not on the street.

You can recycle newspapers and bottles.

They will be collected and used again.

Part 5

There is another important way you can be a good neighbor.

You can work hard on your schoolwork.

You can learn all that you can.

Then you will be able to help others when you grow up.

Measurement

Part 1

Doctors and nurses measure their patients.

Measuring things is very useful in math, science, and medicine. We can measure each other to find out how tall we are. We can find out how much we weigh. We can find out our body temperatures. Doctors and nurses measure us. They record the measurements.

FOLDER

C

Measurement

Part 2

The class measures the weather.

Mrs. Arturo's science class is studying the weather. It is early spring. The class is outside. They are measuring the wind speed, the air temperature, and the amount of rainfall. They use different instruments. They record different units of measure. The wind is blowing at 5 miles per hour. The air is 55 degrees Fahrenheit. The rainfall last night was one inch.

Part 3

There are many ways to measure time.

Most people use a clock to measure minutes and hours. The teacher might use the clock to find out if he has enough time to finish reading a story. The students might want to know how many minutes before it's time for recess. People use the movement of Earth on its axis to measure days, weeks, and months. We use the movement of Earth around the sun to measure years. We write days, weeks, months, and years on a calendar.

Measurement

Part 4

Mrs. Lee's class measures objects.

The students in Mrs. Lee's class are using rulers, meter sticks, and tape measures to measure objects in the classroom. They are recording the length, height, and width of objects. They will compare and contrast their measurements.

Part 5

Mr. Freeman's class is doing experiments with little cars. They want to know if the cars will roll farther if the incline is steeper. On the first run, they set the incline at 8 inches. The red car rolled 17 inches. The blue car rolled 15 inches. The yellow car rolled 14 inches.

Now they will raise the incline to 10 inches. They are ready to begin the second run.

Everyday Objects

Part 1

There are some objects we use at mealtime. It is good to learn the names of those objects. The names help us talk about them.

Everyday Objects

Part 2

Today is Monday, May 2.

We use many different objects in school. We need to know the names of those objects. We need to know how to use them.

Everyday Objects

Part 3

We can use some objects in more than one way. For example, we can use a knife to spread jam. We can also use a knife to cut cake.

Community Workers

Part 1

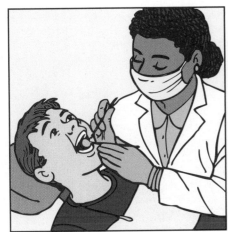  

Many people live in a community. People in a community need many things. Community workers help get the things we need. They help us do the things we need to do. Some community workers are dentists, firefighters, and teachers.

Part 2

Community workers do many different jobs.

Police officers teach people to be safe.

Mail workers get our mail to us.

Farmers grow food for us.

Part 3

  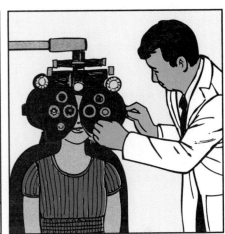

Community workers do things for other people. They talk to people. They help people in many ways. Some community workers who help others are waiters, babysitters, and doctors.

Part 4

Community workers are important. They make things we need. They do jobs we need to have done. Without community workers, our community would not be a good place to live.

Part 5

You see community workers almost everywhere you go. They help you in many ways. Think about times community workers have helped you.

Part 1

Some animals live in the woods.

One kind of animal is a mammal. Dogs and cats are mammals. Rabbits and deer are mammals. Bears and people are mammals. What is a mammal? How are these animals the same?

Part 2

Dogs and people are mammals.

Mammals are animals that have live babies. Baby mammals drink their mother's milk. Mammals do not lay eggs. Mammals have hair or fur. Mammals do not have feathers or scales. Mammals breathe air. Mammals have warm bodies, even when it is cold.

Part 3

Some animals are mammals and some are not.

Mammals have hair and breathe air. Mammals have live babies. Mammal mothers make milk for their babies to drink. Birds are not mammals. Fish are not mammals. Snakes are not mammals. Deer *are* mammals. Deer live in a group called a herd.

Part 4

Nocturnal animals are active at night.

At night, some animals go to sleep and some animals are awake. Animals that are active at night are called nocturnal animals. Some nocturnal mammals are deer, bears, rabbits, mice, and cats. The owl is a nocturnal bird.

Part 5

Nocturnal animals use their senses to get around in the dark.

Some nocturnal animals, like owls and cats, can see very well in the dark. Other nocturnal creatures, like deer and mice, have very good hearing. Bears use their excellent sense of smell to find food.

NOTES

NOTES